DATE DUE

APR 1 0 1995			
GAYLORD			PRINTED IN U.S.A.

JOHN F. KENNEDY
and the Young People of America

Also by BILL ADLER

The Kennedy Wit

Kids' Letters to President Kennedy

The Churchill Wit

Love Letters to the Mets

Love Letters to the Beatles

Dear President Johnson

Boys Are Very Funny People

Letters from Camp

JOHN F. KENNEDY

and the
Young People of America

Compiled and Edited by

BILL ADLER
Author of THE KENNEDY WIT

DAVID McKAY COMPANY, INC.
New York

JOHN F. KENNEDY

AND THE YOUNG PEOPLE OF AMERICA

Library of Congress Catalog Card Number: 65-24700

MANUFACTURED IN THE UNITED STATES OF AMERICA

TO

The young people of America who have dedicated themselves to keeping John F. Kennedy's fine ideals and magnificent principles alive for generations to come.

Contents

Introduction

The letters in this book were sent by children and young people to John F. Kennedy and to his wife, Jacqueline Kennedy.

They record the warm, wonderful affection and high regard that young America had for the thirty-fifth President of the United States.

It is fair to say that no President in our history so captured the hearts of our youth from Maine to Hawaii.

John F. Kennedy was *their* President—young, vibrant, courageous, full of spirit and good humor.

They thought of him as one of them. This first President born in the twentieth century. This young President with two small children. This handsome American who had youthful grace and charm, whether at a state dinner, at a press conference, or on a football field.

John F. Kennedy, heroic wartime commander of a PT boat, and Pulitzer-Prize-winning author, was a shining example of the new breed of leaders who truly belonged to young America.

These letters show a love for a man, father and President, as only young people can express it with candor and delightful originality.

John F. Kennedy and the Young People of America serves to remind all of us that John F. Kennedy will not be forgotten by that generation of Americans destined to carry on the work he so magnificently began.

BILL ADLER
NEW YORK CITY

JOHN F. KENNEDY
and the Young People of America

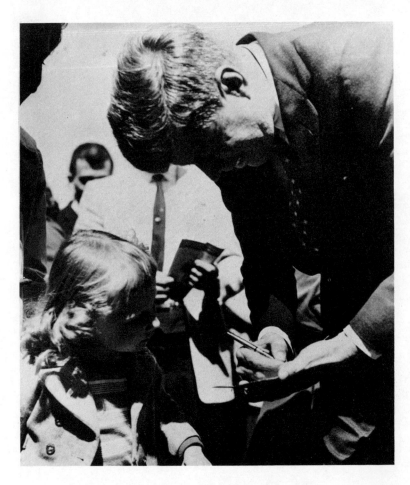

Wheeling, West Virginia, April 19, 1960. An unidentified young girl added Senator John F. Kennedy's autograph to her collection as the Democratic Presidential hopeful stopped outside an industrial plant here to sign autographs. He was greeted by many well-wishers on his whirlwind tour of West Virginia.

PART 1.

From Young Hearts with Love to
John F. Kennedy

Dear President Kennedy,

You have done a lot of great things since you became President. I think the greatest thing is the Peace Corps.

I would like to join the Peace Corps and work in a faraway country but I can't do it yet. I'm not even allowed to cross the street by myself.

Newport, R.I.

A friend,
Barry K.

Dear President Kennedy,

I have been practicing so I can talk like you do.

I stand in front of the mirror and make believe I am JFK.

When my friends come over to the house, I read your speeches and ask them to close their eyes and then I say, "Who do I sound like?"

I did it yesterday and one of my friends said, "Nixon." So I sent him home.

Philadelphia, Pa.

Your friend,
Roy P.

Dear President Kennedy,

They should put your picture on a postage stamp. We don't have any stamps as good-looking as you.

If they had your picture on a stamp, the government would make lots of money because everybody would send more letters.

Please make it a 1¢ stamp so children can afford it.

Houston, Tex.

Sincerely,
Dale E.

John F. Kennedy, Jr., peered from his secret door in his father's Presidential desk while the President glanced over some papers in his White House office. This photo was taken late in the day, and John-John, already in his pajamas and bathrobe, was enjoying a final romp with his father before bed.

Dear Mr. President,

Last week I got a new sailboat and I call it PT-109 just like your boat.

Friday I took my PT-109 to sail it in the lake and it sank just like your PT-109.

Yours,

Brooklyn, N.Y. Dennis K.

Dear Mr. President,

Here is my picture. Would you please hang it in the White House? It would make me the most famous kid in my school.

Yours truly,

Tulsa, Okla. Arnold B.

Dear Mr. President,

I think you have done a lot of good things as President of the USA but there is one thing I don't like.

I heard that you may send a dog to the moon first. I don't think you should do that. I think you should send a man to the moon first. A good dog is hard to find.

Yours truly,

Des Moines, Iowa Benjamin B.

Dear Mr. Kennedy,

Here is good news. I have decided to write you a different letter every day.

This is letter number one. In every letter, I will give you all the news from my school friends and Girl Scout troop.

I will keep writing every day until I run out of news. When I run out of news, Marcia will write you so you won't miss anything.

Goodbye from letter number one. Look for letter number two tomorrow.

Love,

New York City Nancy H.

Dear Mr. President,

Everybody calls you JFK. I wish everybody would call me HBL. That stands for Horace Bud Lamston. But they don't. They just call me Bud. How can I get them to call me HBL like they call you JFK? I am getting tired of just plain Bud.

Best wishes to JFK,

Chicago, Ill.   From HBL

Dear President Kennedy,

Do you think you could get federal aid for our team? We need bats, balls and a few good players.

We are true, loyal JFK men.

Jeff L., Team Captain

Pittsburgh, Pa.

Dear President Kennedy,

I don't think anybody has ever done this before and I would like to be the first one.

I would like to start a museum of old clothes from Presidents.

Do you have any old clothes you are not wearing any more? As long as they are not ripped and are clean, I will put them in my old-clothes-from-Presidents museum.

Thank you,

Los Angeles, Calif.   Jeffrey L.

P.S. If you see ex-Presidents Eisenhower and Truman, please ask them if they have any old clothes for the museum.

Dear Mr. Kennedy,

How can I get out of this neighborhood? There isn't a Democrat on my block.

A loyal Democrat,

Portland, Me.   Randolph K.

7

One hundred members of the Girls Nation visited the White House in August 1963 to present President Kennedy with an honorary membership in their organization. The President quipped, "You are more beautiful than the governors." He went on to explain that the week before he had accepted an honorary membership in the Boys Nation and had remarked that they showed more initiative than the governors then meeting in Florida. The President then commented, "That remark got me into a great deal of difficulty."

Members of the famed Vienna Boys
Choir, clad in sailors' uniforms, enter-
tained President Kennedy with a concert
in the White House Rose Garden on January 9, 1962. The Choir was winding up
a three-month tour of the United States.
They had previously sung for President
and Mrs. Kennedy at St. Stephen's Church
during the First Family's state visit
to Vienna in June of the previous year.

Dear President Kennedy,

Could you fix it so Kennedy fans don't have to pay taxes?

My father voted for you and likes you very much. If you could do this, it would show all the people who are for you how much you appreciate them.

It would also make Nixon fans very jealous.

Truly yours,
Olympia, Wash.   Hilton W.

Dear President John F. Kennedy,

I saw your movie *PT-109*. You were a great war hero but I hope you won't be upset if I tell you that you weren't such a great actor in the picture.

I know you are busy but I think you should brush up on your acting.

A real and true friend,
Knoxville, Tenn.   Jean J.

Dear President Kennedy,

I bet it is very hard to be President of the United States. I bet you get real tired. I know because my father is a taxi driver and he gets tired all the time.

Your friend,
North Hollywood, Calif.   Rufus W.

Dear President John F. Kennedy,

I wrote "I Like JFK" on the blackboard in my class when the teacher was out of the room.

When she came back into the room, she made me erase it from the blackboard.

I think my teacher is a Republican.

Best,
Honolulu, Hawaii   Arnold S.

Dear Mr. President,

Whenever you have lots and lots of troubles, just remember that all the kids in America are for you and kids are better than grownups for cheering up troubled people.

Sincerely,

St. Louis, Mo.   Simon H.

Dear President Kennedy,

I am a kid. I am eleven. I am a nobody. Do you ever write to say hello to nobodies? This nobody would like you to.

Herbert R.

New York City

Dear JFK,

How come they don't give medals to Presidents?

You should get one. If they don't give you one, I will make you a medal out of a tin can cover.

Write me and tell me and I will come to Washington and give you the first medal any President ever got.

Your friend,

Trenton, N.J.   Kevin K.

P.S. Tin cans make good-looking medals.

To the President of the United States, John F. Kennedy
From Michael Wexton

Every year, the President throws out the first ball of the major league baseball season. This year it would be nice if the President threw out the first ball of our Babe Ruth League in Omaha.

Wouldn't you like to be the first President in history to do it?

The Babe Ruth League may not be as important as the major leagues but we try hard.

Please come,
Michael

During the heated West Virginia primary in May, 1960, Senator John F. Kennedy paused in a day of hectic campaigning to chat with two non-voting Huntington fans, Linda Bodo and Bucky Mullins.

Hi JFK,

I liked you when you were a Senator. I like you when you are a President. I like you on TV and I like you in person. I like you in the morning. I like you in the night. But I can't like you after 9 o'clock. I am asleep.

A pal,
Mickey K.

Parkersburg, W. Va.

Dear Mr. President,

This is the first letter I am writing on my new typewriter. I got the typewriter for my birthday and I wanted to send the first letter to you.

Please excuse any mistakes in this letter because the tyewriter doesn't type so good yet.

Love,
Barbara S. (Age 11)

Doylestown, Pa.

Hi Mr. President,

You know any good names for a dog? I just got a new poodle and I don't know what to call him.

My sister thinks we should call him Pinky but I don't think so because Pinky isn't a good name for a boy dog and he isn't even pink. He is brown.

I told my sister I would write to you because you are the President and you know a lot about people and dogs.

Your friend,
Curtis A.

Wilmington, Del.

P.S. If you think Pinky is a good name, please don't write back.

Dear Mr. President,
I have written a story for you.

A Special Man

Once upon a time there was a man who everybody liked a lot. Children liked him and grownups liked him. He was very good-looking and he wrote a famous book which everyone read, except the children who were too young and didn't know how to read yet.

This man was a hero in the war and won a medal for what he did. He was a sailor but not a regular sailor. He was an officer.

After the war, he became a Senator. All the people from his state voted for him because they liked him. Only the children didn't vote for him because they were too young to vote. But the children liked him, too.

Then one day, this man ran for President of the United States and he won the election and he became President. Everybody was very happy that he was President especially the children because they liked him best of all.

So this man moved into the White House with his pretty wife and two small children. He did a lot of good things in the White House for his country and everybody said he was a terrific President.

And the children said he was terrific even though they didn't understand everything.

This is my story about a special man.

The End

Love,
Cincinnati, Ohio   Molly B.

P.S. This is a story about you, Mr. President. Did you guess it was?

Only a child could upstage the President. Here Mr. Kennedy paused during a ceremony in October, 1962, in which he presented the Harmon Aviation Trophy, to recognize a young man who had become enthralled with the trophy. The boy is John Ross, age 5. The young ladies are Marla Lee Prather, 7, and Jane Ross, 7.

Senator John F. Kennedy reached high over the heads of adults to shake hands with a small boy outside his Hyannis Port home, during a brief rest from the grueling campaign trail in July, 1960.

Dear JFK,

If I have another brother, I hope my parents name him after you.

I have five brothers already and I told my mother my idea but she said five brothers is enough.

Your good pal,
Westport, Conn.   Lawrence H.

Dear President Kennedy,

I need pictures of JFK.

We are having a contest to see who can get the most pictures of you and Billy Reed has 82. I want to win and I only have 9 pictures of you.

Please send 100 more right away.

Your pal,
South Bend, Ind.   Richard C.

P.S. I hope you don't want Billy to win.

Hello President Kennedy,

This is hello from Mickey Albert, your friend from Houston, Texas.

You are the best man in the 50 states because nobody can boss you around. You are lucky that nobody can boss you around.

I am 12 and I have a hundred bosses. Everybody bosses me around.

Love,
Mickey

Dear President Kennedy,

When did you know you were going to be the Pres of the whole USA? How old were you when you knew?

I am nine and I know already.

A future Pres of the USA,
Milwaukee, Wis.   Ronnie F.

Dear Mr. President,

Does the USA make any lucky pennies? Does my friend, the President of the United States, have any?

I have 18 pennies but they aren't lucky.

Your friend,

New York City

Mona D.

Dear President Kennedy,

I heard that you were a very fast reader. I am a very fast reader, too. I am the fastest reader in my class because when I read, I skip a lot of pages.

Yours truly,

Kansas City, Kan.

Jay G.

P.S. How long did it take you to read this letter? It took me 15 seconds but it was easy for me because I wrote it.

Dear President Kennedy,

Here is a copy of our school paper. Look on the front page. They wrote a big story all about you. Next to the big story about you is a big story about me and my butterfly collection. I am very proud to have my story next to your story.

Sincerely,

Colorado Springs, Colo.

Alex H.

P.S. I am the editor of the paper.

Dear Mr. Kennedy,

I have written you a secret message.

If you want to read my secret message, hold this piece of paper over a candle in the dark. If you don't have a candle, send this piece of paper to J. Edgar Hoover and the FBI and they will tell you my secret message. That is their job.

Yours truly,

Greenville, N.C.

Artie S.

John F. Kennedy, Jr., at the ripe age of 18 months, practiced his walking in the most important office in the world, the White House, while his proud father looked on. The date was May 28, 1962.

Dear Mr. President,

What is the best way to become President without studying arithmetic, spelling and geography? A friend of mine wants to know.

Allentown, Pa.

Your pal,
Rick L.

Dear President Kennedy,

I am writing to you because I know that you help people—even kids.

What is my problem? I will tell you. It is money. I can't live on my allowance any more. My cost of living has gone up. I am a depressed area. Help!

Malden, Mass.

Love,
Frank G.

Dear President JFK,

All of us kids are for your physical fitness program.

We want to help. Here is our idea. More people would go for your physical fitness program if you had some exercises that everybody could do in bed.

Raleigh, N.C.

Your friend,
Leonard S.

Dear President Kennedy,

I took your book *Profiles in Courage* out of the library. I read it six times and had the book out of the library for three weeks.

I had to pay the library fourteen cents extra because I kept it out so long.

Could you send me the fourteen cents since it was your book?

Endicott, N.Y.

Yours,
Laurie G.

Dear Mr. President,
   I love you. I am sending you a postcard because we are very poor and we can't afford stamps.
   I saved for two weeks to buy this postcard.

Wheeling, W. Va.

Love forever,
Mary H.

P.S. It's no fun when you are poor.

Dear President Kennedy,
   Why don't you challenge Khrushchev to a game of touch football?
   That would scare the Russians forever and ever.

St. Joseph, Mo.

Best wishes,
Hattie C.

Dear Mr. President,
   Last week, I broke my arm. I have my arm in a cast. Would you sign my cast?
   I never broke my arm before and it would be a big thrill.
   Please say yes now. I don't know if I will ever break my arm again.

Lansing, Mich.

Thank you,
Lincoln H.

Dear Mr. President,
   I saw you on TV when you threw out the first ball of the baseball season.
   Was it a curve ball? A sinker? Or a fast ball?
   It is a good thing you are President because you could never be a baseball player.

Denver, Colo.

Yours truly,
Alan L.

President Kennedy gave a framed citation to Andrew S. Roberts of Flushing, New York, after presenting the boy with a gold lifesaving medal. The twelve-year-old lad, a school-crossing guard at Public School 214 in Flushing, was honored for pulling two small children from the path of a speeding automobile. The photograph was taken at the White House on May 9, 1963. Standing beside President Kennedy during the ceremony was Sen. Kenneth Keating of New York.

Dear President Kennedy,

You are a good President. You are helping the poor people. You should help all the poor people. Start with the A's.

Huntsville, Ala.

Sincerely,
Louise A.

Dear Mr. President,

We all think you are a terrific President except for one thing.

Yesterday in the newspapers you said that everybody should drink lots of milk.

Couldn't you say everybody should drink lots of ice cream sodas and Cokes? Give us a break.

Gainesville, Ga.

Your pals,
Richard, Jack, Larry, Mike

Dear Mr. President,

I am keeping a scrapbook of everything you did every day since you became President. But one day is missing.

What exactly did you do on February 18, 1962? Please start with breakfast and go through supper. This is an important historical record for my Boy Scout troop.

Chicago, Ill.

Sincerely,
Albert B.

Dear President Kennedy,

I like your face. I like your face best when you are mad. Like the face you made when the Russians put the missiles in Cuba.

You scared the Russians with your mad face but not us. We know you were only acting.

Albany, N.Y.

A good American,
Jennifer R.

Dear Mr. President Kennedy,

I heard on TV that you can't get enough money from Congress.

Why don't you do what my brother and I do when our father won't give us enough money for our allowance.

We make faces and stamp our feet. Sometimes we cry. It always works.

Your pals,

Sioux City, Iowa   David and Ira L.

Dear Mr. President,

We named our football team the JFK football team. We have a good team but we just lost five games in a row and we are going to change the name of our team so we won't embarrass the President of the United States.

Sincerely,

Glen Cove, N.Y.   Howard R.

Dear President Kennedy,

I would like to visit the New Frontier.

Could you please send me the address?

Yours truly,

Chattanooga, Tenn.   Richard C.

Dear President Kennedy,

When you won the election, my father proposed a toast to you at dinner.

Everybody toasted you. Even me. I toasted you with water. I had to drink four glasses of water to keep up with the grown-ups.

Love,

Olympia, Wash.   Harriet B.

27

President Kennedy received a paper-weight and a report to the nation from a group of 4-H Club delegates who called at the White House on March 7, 1961, in observance of National 4-H Club Week. The 4-H members, from left to right, were William Platt III of Gainesville, Fla.; Frances McQueen of Craig, Mo.; Robert Barr of Port Matilda, Pa.; Joyce Finnel of Cleveland, Tenn.; Howard Wefkeiser of Kewanee, Ill.; and Kendra Lane of Clements, Calif. Also present was Secretary of Agriculture Orville Freeman.

When President Kennedy arrived at the Laramie, Wyoming airport in September, 1963, he was met by a group of Wyoming Boy Scouts who demonstrated the Scout oath to the President. He was to give a speech at the University of Wyoming.

Dear President Kennedy,

How come since you are President of the USA, you aren't stuck-up or conceited?

My boyfriend, Roger, is president of his class and you can't even talk to him.

Yours truly,

Linden, N.J.   Betsey W.

Dear JFK,

When is your birthday? I want to send you a surprise present.

What do you like that doesn't cost more than thirteen cents?

Love,

Oakland, Calif.   Shirley T.

Dear President Kennedy,

My name is Mark. I am nine. I'll bet you never heard of me but I heard of you.

That is why I am writing this letter. Now we are even. Now you heard of me.

Best wishes,

New York City   Mark L.

Dear Mr. President Kennedy,

We had a masquerade party at my school and I came looking like you. I looked pretty good. A lot of kids said I was a terrific President Kennedy but I didn't win first prize. I won second prize. Stuart Wilson won first prize. He came looking like Mickey Mantle. It wasn't fair. Nobody could beat Mickey Mantle.

Best,

Valley Forge, Pa.   Eric L.

Hello Mr. President,

How much did your campaign for President cost?

I just ran for president of my class and it cost me all the money I have. I spent 93¢ for signs, 42¢ for cardboard and 19¢ for paint.

I know it cost you more but at least you won.

Sincerely,

Cheyenne, Wyo.   Herbert R.

Dear President Kennedy,

I saved my allowance to send you a box of candy for your birthday.

I hope you like it. Happy Birthday.

Holly W.

Santa Barbara, Calif.

P.S. I ate two pieces before I mailed the candy. It is delicious.

Dear President John Kennedy,

I am saving all my money so I can come to Washington to meet you.

I live in Kansas. So far, I have 39¢. How much more money do I need?

Love,
Barbara L.

Dear President Kennedy,

Last night I had a dream. And in this dream, you called me on the telephone and asked me to fly with you in your airplane *Air Force 1*.

I know it sounds silly to ask but you didn't happen to have the same dream, did you?

A pal,

Columbus, Ohio   Arthur G.

Arriving at the United States Military
Academy at West Point to address the
graduating class on June 6, 1962, the
President greeted three cadets whom he
appointed to the Academy when he was
a United States Senator from Massachusetts. The three cadets, from left to
right, were Peter Oldfield of Cohasset,
Mass.; David Binney of Wrentham, Mass.;
and Kevin Renachan of Hingham, Mass.

President Kennedy reviewed an honor guard of cadets upon his arrival at the Military Academy to address the 1962 graduating class and present diplomas to the top thirty West Point graduates.

Dear President Kennedy,

Did you know your name was a household word like Crackerjack and Coke ?

Forest Hills, N.Y.

Your friend,
Ray J.

Dear President Kennedy,

In my honest opinion, a lot of people didn't vote for you during the election because you are so handsome. Sometimes people don't trust people who are very good-looking. I know. I ran for vice-president of my class and I lost. I am very good-looking.

Scott F.

Racine, Wis.

Dear President Kennedy,

I have seen lots of pictures of you shaking hands with kids.

Boy, do I wish I could get to shake hands with you just once. I wouldn't wash that hand again as long as I live.

A pal,
Michael N.

Marion, Ohio

Dear President JFK,

All the children in the USA are behind JFK 100%.

They have always been for you and they always will be for you.

You could do a big favor for all the children in the USA who are a hundred per cent for you.

All you have to do is announce that on July 8, it will be *Be Kind to Children Day*. We sure could use it.

Sincerely,
David L.

Dayton, Ohio

Dear President Kennedy,
   You know what my favorite picture of you is?
They haven't even taken it yet.
   My favorite picture of you is with me.

San Francisco, Calif.

Love and kisses,
Betty G.

Dear President Kennedy,
   Would you please make a law that will make 60 the passing grade in arithmetic. Please do it by next Wednesday. That is when I have my test.

Akron, Ohio

Thank you,
Mickey L.

Dear President Kennedy,
   We just elected you a member of our secret club. Please send sixty cents for your dues.

Seattle, Wash.

Your friend,
Harold B.

P.S. The regular dues is seventy-five cents. This is a special rate.

Dear President Kennedy,
   I heard from my teacher that you are having trouble balancing the budget.
   My mother has the same problem.

Lansing, Mich.

Your pal,
Arlene S.

President Kennedy talked to the Andrews
Air Force Base All-Stars, as he changed
at the base from a helicopter to his
jet plane for a weekend visit with his
family at Hyannis Port in August, 1963.
The President holds a boxed baseball,
which he then autographed for the team,
the Air Force Little League champions.

President Kennedy chatted in his White
House office on March 5, 1963, with the
two winners of an essay contest sponsored by the Department of Labor. The
contest, on youth's challenge in the
labor market of the 1960s, was held in
connection with the Department's 50th
anniversary. The winners were Richard
Frazier of Flushing, N.Y., a student at
Queens College, and Carla Lipsig from
Waltham, Mass., of Brandeis University.

A young boy perched atop a fence post appeared to be the only calm observer as President Kennedy arrived at the Ashland, Wisconsin, airport in September, 1963, after having flown over the nearby Apostle Islands in Lake Superior.

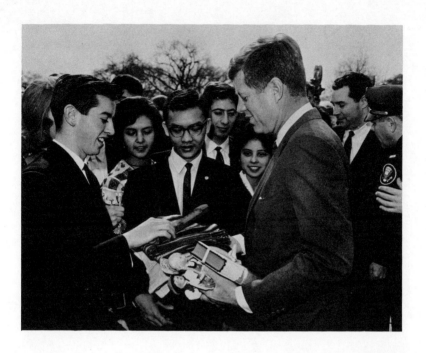

Foreign students visiting the United States as delegates to the New York Herald Tribune Youth Forum presented the President with gifts from many lands. A young Bolivian student added a wooden flute to the pile of presents.

PART 2.

Teen-age America

Dear President Kennedy,

Tuesday we had to write a composition in my English class about an American President and I wrote about you. Yesterday I received my paper back and I was marked C—.

My friend, Richard Huber, wrote about Lincoln and he was marked A—, and Jerry Holmes wrote about Jefferson and he was marked B+.

Don't feel badly. I would have received a C— even if I had written about Lincoln or Jefferson. I am the worst writer in the class except for Peter Henderson. He wrote about Taft and got a D.

Yours truly,
Woonsocket, R.I.   Andrew G.

Dear President Kennedy,

I think it is wonderful that you spend plenty of time with your children even though you are very busy as President.

Every parent should spend a lot of time with their children even if we are a pain in the neck sometimes.

Your friend,
New York City   Mickey H. (Age 16)

Dear President Kennedy,

My father said that you have made the world a better place to live so could you please do something about my neighborhood?

William W.

Queens, New York

Among the crowd of 13,000 people who turned out at Indianapolis' Coliseum on October 4, 1960, for a campaign speech by Senator John F. Kennedy were these enthusiastic young people, members of Young Democrats of Indiana University.

President Kennedy applauded 17-year-old
Mary Ann Kingry at White House ceremonies in June, 1962, when Mary Ann
was awarded a medal for exceptional service in the Junior Red Cross. The President
commented, "The Vice President recently
predicted we would someday have a
woman President. I want to say it seems to
me we have a promising candidate here."

President Kennedy kept a 15-month-old promise by greeting the senior class of Tomah, Wisconsin, High School in the White House Rose Garden June 7, 1961. While campaigning in Wisconsin in 1960, Mr. Kennedy had invited the students to visit him in Washington and they took him up on it. In this photograph, class member Ronald Lowe, a Winnebago Indian, gave the President a basket woven for the occasion by his mother.

Dear President Kennedy,

You have been my inspiration. Before you became President, it was my ambition to go into my father's business. My father makes umbrellas.

Now I want to go into politics and I hope someday I can be President.

My father is not enthusiastic about the idea. He believes making umbrellas is a more practical ambition.

Boston, Mass.

Respectfully,
Richard F., Boston College

Dear President Kennedy,

I don't know why I like you so much but I just do.

Most of the time when you like a person very much, you don't really know why. It is just a feeling that you have about the other person. You may like them because of the way they smile or the way they talk or even the way they walk or look. If you try to figure out why you like them, it won't do you any good. You just like them.

So I hope you don't mind, Mr. President, if I can't tell you why. It is just one of those things.

Brooklyn, N.Y.

Love,
May G.
Tilden High School

Dear President Kennedy,

You know what I would like? I would like you to come to our spring dance and be my date. Wouldn't that be keen?

We will have a real swinging combo playing at our dance. They are called The Hipsters.

You'll have a real ball, Mr. President, and it will help you forget all your troubles with Castro.

I am a keen dancer and I always let the boy lead.

Madison, Wis.

Love,
Babs A.

48

Dear President Kennedy,

There are thousands of children all over the country who would like to meet you.

Maybe you should take a week off from work and travel around the country and meet the children.

It would be very good for their morale.

I am not one of the children. I am a teenager.

Amy L.

New Haven, Conn.

Dear President Kennedy,

It is my honest opinion that your inauguration speech is one of the four best speeches by an American President.

The other three were Washington's farewell to his troops, Lincoln's Gettysburg Address and President Roosevelt's first inauguration address.

Your words "Ask not what your country can do for you but what you can do for your country" will rank with FDR's "We have nothing to fear but fear itself."

I know that this is only the opinion of one teenager but I did plenty of hard thinking about this and I read many speeches over and over again before I wrote this letter.

Yours sincerely,

Allentown, Pa.   Elliot H.

Dear Mr. President,

I have been running for president of my class but I haven't won yet. Every time I think I am going to win somebody comes along and beats me.

Could you give me some hints on how to win an election? You have never lost and I have lost three years in a row.

If I don't win an election soon, I may quit trying. I am going broke buying posters and buttons.

Your truly,
Sonny W.

Freeport, N.Y.   Freeport High School

49

Patricia Webber and her twin sister, Paula, of Sumter, South Carolina, were the 1961 National Easter Seal twins. They joined television personality Art Linkletter in a visit to present the President with Easter seals and Easter baskets for the two Kennedy children. Joseph J. Foss, President, Society for Crippled Children and Adults, looked on.

President Kennedy received a wild and
enthusiastic greeting from young pupils
whose meeting with the President at the
White House was a thrill of a lifetime.

Dear Mr. President,

Last week we had an election in our school for class president. We all thought that Jimmy Reeves would win the election because he was class president last year and he did a good job. But he didn't win.

Some kid named Howie Kennedy won. He had signs all over school that said "Vote for Kennedy."

I believe he only ran for election because he knew that everybody would vote for a Kennedy.

He was lucky that all the kids are for President Kennedy. He was really riding to victory on your coat tails.

Sincerely,
Harold S.

Lawrence, N.Y.   Lawrence High School

Dear Mr. President,

Every time I read a newspaper I get very upset. All I see in the paper is war news. There seems to be fighting all over the world. When I get very upset and scared about the news, I have a good way of not being scared. I think about you and I tell myself that John F. Kennedy is our President and he is strong and smart.

Thank you for taking care of everything.

Carol B.

Alexandria, Va.

Dear Mr. President,

Do you have any leftover Kennedy-for-President buttons from the 1960 election?

I have some Nixon-for-President buttons because there were plenty of them left.

Thank you very much,
Julie H.

Cleveland, Ohio   Central High School

52

Dear President Kennedy,

I think your program of aid to education, the Peace Corps, and medicare is terrific. It will be good for all the people.

I hope you don't mind my saying so, Mr. President, but not enough young people understand your program. It is important that young people understand it because they are the ones that can explain it to their parents.

If you let me come down to Washington to see you, you could explain your program to me and then I could explain it to all the kids I know in Chicago and they could explain it to their parents.

It would be a real help to you because nobody knows more kids in Chicago than me.

Yours truly,
Eugene L. (Age 15)

Dear JFK,

Boy, is it keen to have a President who isn't square. All the kids in my class say you are a real swinger. I hope you aren't upset. It is a compliment to be called a swinger. It is cool.

Maybe they won't ever call you a swinger in the history books but to us you will always be the chief swinger of the USA.

Love and kisses,

New York City   Diane A.

Dear Mr. President,

I ran for president of the junior class in my high school. I had to make a speech and I used one of your speeches that I read in the newspaper. It was one of your best speeches. I changed a few words. Everybody said you would have been proud of me if you heard my speech. I lost the election.

Sincerely,

Chicago, Ill.   Alex N.

Little Karima Khalil, the daughter of a United Arab Republic couple studying in the United States, seemed unimpressed to be on stage with the President of the United States as she romped up the White House stairs while Mr. Kennedy greeted Fulbright exchange students. She headed for the President's office, top left, only to be retrieved by Frances Adams, student conference secretary. Another try, upper right, ended also in capture.

Dear Mr. President Kennedy,

I am sending you a package. In that package is my high school album. Most of my friends have signed my album but none of the kids in my class had their albums signed by anyone important. Oh, one of the girls had a disc jockey from the radio station sign her album but he is just a disc jockey.

Do you think you could sign my album? Write anything you want. If you are stuck for something to say, ask one of your speech writers to help you. I doubt if you need a speech writer. You are terrific with words.

Please look for my package when it comes. I wrote "Rita's Album" on the wrapping paper with my magic marker so it will be easier to find.

When you get the album, you will see that my friends wrote goofy and silly sayings. Don't pay any attention to what they wrote. Whatever JFK writes will be sensational. Even if it is only one word.

Love,
Sweetwater, Tex.   Rita B.

Dear Mr. President,

You have done a lot for this country since you became President but there is one more little item that you could do that would be a big help to kids who are 17 like me.

It has to do with our allowance. We don't get enough to get along. Just to take a girl to a movie and for a hamburger takes your whole week's allowance. Right now I think I owe my father so much money that I may not get my allowance for 10 years.

If you could make allowances a tax deduction, it would encourage our parents to give us more. Frankly, the government won't be losing much money because we don't get that much money anyway.

You would be a big hero with all the kids if you could do it.

Yours,
Mobile, Ala.   Andy W.

56

Dear President Kennedy,

I want to congratulate you on your program to get more women into the government.

Women can do a good job for their country and they are more reliable than men. America would be a hundred percent better if we had more women in high positions. If you had a woman as Secretary of the Treasury, you would never have any trouble balancing the budget because women know how to watch the pennies.

All the women are for your program and so are the men who know what is best for the country.

Yours very truly,

Baltimore, Md.   Marilyn F.

Dear Mr. President,

You have done more for the teenagers than any other President. I have thought about it and I think that the reason is that you can remember what it is like to be a teenager because you were a teenager not so long ago yourself.

Most of our other Presidents were too old to remember how you feel when you are sixteen or seventeen. Grownups forget. Even my brother can't understand and he is twenty-three.

Thank you, Mr. President, for remembering us.

Sincerely yours,

Baton Rouge, La.   Hannah L.

Dear President Kennedy,

I wrote a campaign song for you. I called my song "Give Your Vote to JFK."

I sang the song for my friends and they told me that if I sang the song it would get votes for Nixon.

Now you know why you won. It was because I kept quiet.

Very truly,

Tucson, Ariz.   Ogden H. (Age 14)

It may not be the most important thing for a political candidate to know, but Senator John F. Kennedy, visiting Squaw Valley, was taught how to make a proper snowball by a six-year-old named John and a five-year-old named Debbie. The youngsters did not seem especially awed to be instructing a future U.S. President.

Astronaut Walter Schirra, Jr., took his
family to the White House in October,
1962, to meet the President. Kennedy
learned from Suzanne Schirra that she
was five and went to "kinneygarten."

Young people were always sending gifts
to President Kennedy. Barbara Behm had
the unique opportunity of presenting
her gift in person. As the President's
private plane was about to leave West
Palm Beach, Florida, for Washington,
the nine-year-old young lady gave the
President two ducks for Caroline's
birthday, which he was happy to accept.

Dear President Kennedy,

I am a freshman in high school and I like to ask questions. I was curious to know why you don't play as much golf as Mr. Eisenhower did when he was President.

Is it because you don't play as well as President Eisenhower or do you like other sports better? If so, what sports do you like?

Also what do you like to read most? Is it your speeches or do you like to read other things too?

How about food? Do you like typical American food like hamburgers, hot dogs and french fries or do you go for fancy food like goulash and lobster?

As you can see, I am a girl who likes to ask questions. I hope you are a President who likes to answer them.

Best regards,

Reno, Nev.   Nina B.

Dear Mr. President,

We have just started a Celebrity of the Month Club in my class in high school in Chicago.

We pick a different celebrity every month and write to him. So far it has been:

January	Paul Anka
February	Rock Hudson
March	Elvis
April	Bobby Vinton
May	Tommy Sands
June	Dick Van Dyke

I have suggested your name for July but I don't know if you will be it because all the girls have to vote on the celebrity and there is plenty of competition. I will let you know if you make it for July.

Love,

Chicago, Ill.   Melissa B.

Dear President John Kennedy,

I was wondering if you might need a teenage assistant. You see, a teenage assistant could be a big help in your work with young people.

You have a lot of work already with Castro, the Russians and other problems and an assistant could take the teenage worry off your shoulders.

You should pick a smart teenage assistant.

Yours truly,

Council Bluffs, Iowa   Alan M.

P.S. It so happens I am a teenager with all A's on my report card.

Dear President Kennedy,

You don't have to worry about anything. If the adults ever leave you and go over to the Republican side, we will stand by you.

That is because teenagers are more loyal than grownups. When we like somebody we stick with him forever. We are not what you would call fair-weather friends, like some people.

I don't know exactly how many teenagers there are in America but I do know that nothing can change them from being 100% JFK fans.

Your friend,

Omaha, Neb.   Lincoln N.

Dear President Kennedy,

I think it is great the way you tell Khrushchev off.

I do the same with my kid brother.

A pal,

Grand Rapids, Mich.   Horace G.

Three altar boys of the Sacred Heart
Catholic Church near Palm Springs, Cali-
fornia, received an unexpected thrill
when President Kennedy paused to shake
hands with them as he left church. The
young boys were, from left to right,
Bill Eickelmann, 13; Kevin McGee, 10;
and James Olguin, 11. The priest who
officiated at mass was Father Edwards.

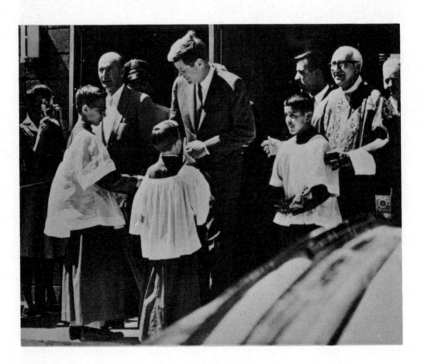

Paying little heed to the falling rain, President Kennedy stopped to chat with students on the White House lawn. The students had come to Washington to take summer jobs in the federal government. In his remarks the President told the students that no career offered so much stimulus as federal government service.

Dear Mr. President,

I hope that someday I will be able to do something great for the USA like you. You have done a lot and I have done nothing. You were a hero in the war and I wasn't. You wrote a book and I haven't. You were a Senator and a President and I haven't been elected anything.

What can I do? You shouldn't be the only one doing things for the good old USA.

A friend,

Duluth, Minn.   Jay S.

P.S. I am thirteen years old and just in high school.

Dear President Kennedy,

My name is Roberta and I am fifteen. I will be sixteen next Thursday (happy birthday to me). It is terrific to be fifteen except for one thing. Parents are always bugging you about the way you dress. I like to wear jeans but my father throws a fit whenever he sees me.

It would be a big help if you could drop my father a note and tell him that jeans are A-OK.

All I would need is the green light from you. My father thinks you are a great dresser for a President.

Your pal,

Washington, D.C.   Roberta B.

Dear President Kennedy,

It would be the biggest thrill of my life if I could come to one of your press conferences. I am a reporter for my school paper but I never get to report anything but football games which we never win.

May I? If you say okay, I promise not to ask any embarrassing questions like the other reporters. I am pro Kennedy.

Sincerely,

Columbia, S.C.   Jerry L.

Dear President Kennedy,

As a sixteen-year-old student from your home town of Boston, I have decided to follow in your footsteps. I hope you don't mind.

What do you feel is the best way to accomplish my goal? Should I become a lawyer or should I be active in my local Democratic Club?

Frankly, I would prefer becoming a statesman without having to be a politician first.

Were you ever a politician? It is hard for me to believe that you ever were. I will always think of you as our statesman President.

Respectfully,

Boston, Mass.   Howard A.

Dear President Kennedy,

I know that this is not the sort of letter that you write to the President of the United States so I hope you will excuse me.

I just had to write this letter. You see, I have nobody to talk over my problems with. My mother works all day and is too tired at night to talk to me. My father is a salesman for a leather company and he isn't home much and I don't have any brothers or sisters. So I am really all alone. I want so badly to talk to somebody smart about this boy I have been dating. I am not sure if he is the right one. I am fourteen and he is eighteen. He is a senior in high school but he doesn't want to go to college even though his parents can afford to send him. He says that college is for squares.

Could you please write, Mr. President, and tell me if I should keep seeing him? I know you are busy with your own problems but I just believe that you are the kind of President who is never too busy for the problems of one of your citizens.

Sincerely,

Hollywood, Calif.   Agnes S.

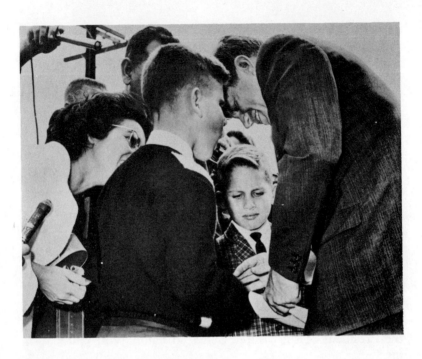

Joey Renzi, an 11-year-old boy from San Diego, has been blind since birth. He was the happiest boy in the world when his dream of meeting President Kennedy came true. Joey gave the President a note he had typed in Braille, thanking the President "for letting me see you at the Marine Corps Recruit Depot"—a day Joey and his family will never forget.

Wildly enthusiastic boys and girls with American flags welcomed the President on his arrival in Galway, Ireland, from Dublin in June, 1963. The nuns and children were from the Convent of Mercy.

Hello Mr. President Kennedy,

You are a great President and you are a great father. The reason you are a great father is you let your daughter Caroline have a pony.

My father is great but he won't let me have a pony or a dog or even a kitten. He likes children but not animals.

I even told him that you let Caroline have a pony but it didn't work. If you would write him a letter and tell how much fun animals are, it might change his mind.

I don't think he would say no to the President.

Your friend,

Mt. Pleasant, Pa.   Ralph E.

Dear President Kennedy,

I am a sophomore in high school. I hope to be a history teacher someday.

I have just made up a list of the ten greatest Presidents and I thought you would be pleased to know that you are number 6.

The first 5 are Lincoln, Washington, FDR, Jefferson and Jackson.

I thought you might want to announce that you are number 6 at your next press conference.

Best regards,

Atlanta, Ga.   Hilton W.

PART 3.

The President and His Family

Dear President Kennedy,

Everybody hates to get up in the morning. Even Presidents. That is why I am writing this letter. In my house, I am the official waker-upper. I always bounce out of bed at 6:30 and shout, "Everybody up!" Sometimes I put a few drops of water on their face if they are still sleeping or I blow my whistle. Nobody ever sleeps after 6:30 in our house.

I would like to come to the White House and do the same thing for you and Mrs. Kennedy. You will never have to worry about getting up ever, ever again.

Love,

New York City   Gloria G.

Dear President Kennedy,

You sure are lucky. No President ever had such a pretty First Lady as you except George Washington who had Martha.

Love,

Meridian, Miss.   Agnes W.

Dear President Kennedy,

I think it is very nice that you gave your brother Robert a job in the government.

Maybe I'll give my brother a job. But it won't be right away because right now I'm not talking to him again.

Jerome R.

Westport, Conn.

73

The young man in this photograph wasn't really a ballet dancer. It was John F. Kennedy, Jr., kissing his father as the President arrived at Otis Air Force Base for a weekend in Hyannis Port, Mass. John-John was flown from the Kennedy summer home on nearby Squaw Island in a helicopter to meet his father's plane.

President and Mrs. Kennedy held a confidential discussion with daughter Caroline aboard the Presidential yacht, the *Honey Fitz*. The yacht picked up the President at Quonset, Rhode Island, after his arrival by plane at the Quonset Point Air Station in October, 1961.

President Kennedy's young son John, Jr., unhappily watched his father prepare to board a plane and go away. He had just been told he couldn't make the trip.

Like every father, John Kennedy enjoyed roughhousing with his children. Here he was at Hyannis Port during November 1961 giving Caroline a piggy-back ride.

Like any dutiful father, John Kennedy helped his daughter with her giant doll as they landed in Hyannis Port, October 1960. A few hours after the photograph was taken, Mr. Kennedy left again to continue his 1960 campaign appearances.

An admiring father applauded his two children, Caroline and John, Jr., as they demonstrated their brand-new dance technique in the President's office. This photo was taken in October, 1962.

The President's young son seemed to be inspecting his father and his father's military aides as President Kennedy arrived at Arlington National Cemetery on November 11, 1963, to pay tribute to America's war dead in the observance of Veterans Day. Walking with the President was General David M. Shoup, then Marine Corps Commandant. Behind the President, from left to right, were his military aides, Major General Chester V. Clifton, Army; Brigadier General Godfrey McHugh, Air Force; and Captain Tazewell T. Shepard, Jr., Navy.

Dear President Kennedy,

We think it is wonderful that you live in the White House with children.

All the kids I know are proud to have children living in the most important house in the world.

Please tell Caroline and John-John that we love them very much and that we are very glad that their father is the President so that they can live in the White House like other kids live in plain houses.

Sincerely,

Pasadena, Calif.   Sharon Y. (Age 12)

My dear President Kennedy,

In my small way, I would like to help you and Mrs. Kennedy because you do so much to help other people.

The way I think I could help you best is to take care of your children, Caroline and John Jr., when you have some place to go.

I am really a very good babysitter and I have had plenty of experience. I have taken care of children in my neighborhood. I usually play games with them and keep them happy. I know that Caroline and John-John will like me as a babysitter.

I charge the parents in my neighborhood 75¢ an hour but for the President and First Lady, I will only charge half price.

Yours truly,

Baltimore, Md.   Freda F.

Dear JFK,

I want to run up to the White House and give you a big kiss and a hug and I don't care if everybody knows it including Mrs. JFK.

I love you,

Los Angeles, Calif.   Beatrice L.

Dear President Kennedy,

I named my cat after you. I call him JFK. I named my canary after Mrs. Kennedy. I call her Jackie. I named my turtle Caroline. I didn't name anything after John Jr. because that's all the pets I have.

Your pal,
Roger H.

Albuquerque, N.M.

Dear Mr. President,

May I please have your permission to marry your daughter Caroline some day. She is very pretty.

I am ten and my mother and father are Democrats. I am going to be a doctor and will make a lot of money from sick people.

Thank you,
Andrew G.

New York City

P.S. I would say that I love Caroline but I don't even know her.

Dear President Kennedy,

I would like to play fullback on the Kennedy football team.

I used to want to play fullback on the New York Giants but I think your team is better.

Bruce R.

New York City

Dear Mr. President,

I'll bet Mrs. Kennedy fell in love with you when she found out that you played touch football.

Women love football players. I'm a baseball player and I don't care if I never get a girl.

Best,
Bobby R.

Nashville, Tenn.

85

Here Caroline Kennedy fondly kissed her father's hand as they entered the Otis Air Force Base hospital to visit Mrs. Kennedy in August 1963. Caroline carried a bouquet of flowers for her mother.

Dear Mr. President Kennedy,

Here is a copy of our school newspaper, *The Trumpet*.

On page three, there is a nice story about you.

It costs $1.00 to get *The Trumpet* for a year. Would you like to buy a subscription? It will be worth it because there will be lots of stories about you.

Maybe Mrs. Kennedy would like a subscription too. Once in a while we write her up.

Bayonne, N.J.

Sincerely,
Agnes H., Editor

PART 4.

Strictly Personal to JFK
from Children Everywhere

Dear Mr. President,
I would like very much a lock of your hair that I can keep in my memory book.
I never asked a President for a lock of his hair before. I was going to ask President Eisenhower but then I saw he didn't have much to spare.

Scarsdale, N.Y.

Thank you in advance,
Jennifer L.

Dear President Kennedy,
How old were you when you made your first mistake?
I am nine and I sure made a lulu yesterday.

Bronx, N.Y.

Your friend,
Ricky L.

Dear Mr. President Kennedy,
How come you don't wear eyeglasses? I thought people who were very smart always wore eyeglasses. You are the only smart person I know who doesn't.

Peoria, Ill.

Yours,
Angela D.

P.S. It so happens I wear eyeglasses.

Dear President Kennedy,
If I ever had another father, I would want it to be you.

San Jose, Calif.

Love,
Naomi L.

Although too young to vote in 1960, Sarah Gowen and March Hutchinson had their own ideas about how Kennedy could win the farm vote. In Washington the candidate posed with the young visitors from Manchester, Iowa. The girls then joined newsmen outside and announced their simple plan to get the farmers on Kennedy's side in the election. "We're going to get our picture taken with him and it will be published in the newspapers back home." They got the picture.

Even a busy President pauses now and
then to sign autographs, especially for
admiring youngsters. Here Mr. Kennedy
received pad and pencil for the purpose
from John Hutson, 9, of Arlington, Va.

Dear President Kennedy,

You have a beautiful speaking voice and your diction and grammar are very good.

I have a nice speaking voice, too except my voice is changing and every once in a while I squeak.

Sincerely,

Baton Rouge, La.   Jay A.

Dear President Kennedy,

How come I didn't get a birthday card from you?

I got a birthday card from my Aunt Martha, my cousin Jack, my Uncle Pete and my friend Amy Lou.

But I didn't get one from you. How come? I am a citizen.

Your friend,

Jacksonville, Fla.   Debby L.

Dear President Kennedy,

I love you. I love you. I love you. I don't care if the whole world knows. Only you I love.

Love,

New York City   Marilyn F.

P.S. Please don't tell my boyfriend, Andy, I sent this letter.

Hi Mr. President,

I wonder if I could ask you for a big favor.

You see, business in my father's shoe store is not too good. I thought if you could work for my father in his store one day a week, it might help business.

If you could do it, please make it on Monday. Monday is the worst day for business.

Thank you,

Green Bay, Wis.   Rita G.

P.S. My father will pay you.

94

Dear President Kennedy,
Here is what I do all week.

Monday	piano lesson
Tuesday	art lesson
Wednesday	dance lesson
Thursday	nothing
Friday	piano lesson
Saturday	nothing
Sunday	Sunday School

What do you do all week? Please send me a list of what you do every day. Put down every day. Even the days when you do nothing.

Reading, Pa.

Your friend,
Donald F.

Hi Mr. Kennedy,
Would the President of the United States like to play a game of marbles with the marble champ of New Rochelle?
Well, I'm it. And I'm ready if you are.

New Rochelle, N.Y.

Yours,
Paul R.

Dear President Kennedy,
You are too handsome to be a President. You should be a rock-and-roll singer.

Brooklyn, N.Y.

Love,
Carole B.

Dear Mr. President Kennedy,
I think you are the best football player we ever had for a President.
Lincoln and Jefferson couldn't even catch a ball.

Muncie, Ind.

Your friend,
Eric A.

This letter was written by seven-year-old Robert F. Kennedy Jr., to his uncle, President Kennedy. Young Bobby decided the best way to see his famous uncle was to write asking for an appointment. He got his appointment, and when he met with the President, solemnly presented him with a salamander named Shadrach.

President Kennedy pinned a lifesaving medal on Wayne Brown of New York City at the White House on May 11, 1962.

Dear President Kennedy,

I would like to come and work for you in Washington.

I am very smart and would be a terrific spy for the FBI.

How much do you pay for spies who are ten years old?

Right now, I make fifty cents a week cleaning around the house so I have to make fifty cents or more.

My brother Bruce says I should be a spy because I am the only one in the family who can keep his mouth shut.

Portland, Me.

Your friend,
Andrew S.

Dear President Kennedy,

My mother says the President of the United States eats hot cereal for breakfast every morning.

Is it true? I don't believe you would do that to us. Write back.

Reading, Pa.

Your pal,
Arthur A.

Dear Mr. President,

What color eyes do you have? Blue, green or brown? I am not sure and they don't teach us that in American History class.

Austin, Tex.

Sincerely,
Nick L.

P.S. I will keep the information a secret if you want. Except my friend, Bobby, who wants to know, too.

Dear Mr. JFK,

The best talker of any President is you.

I like all your famous speeches. The one I like best is the Gettysburg Address.

New York City

Love,
David G.

Dear Mr. President,

I just love your accent. What part of the South are you from?

You-all are great.

Rebecca W.

Jackson, Miss.

Dear President Kennedy,

You are the most handsome President we ever had. Even George Washington wasn't as handsome as you.

I want to paint a picture of your handsome face. Can you send me $3.96 for paint, brush and paper?

It will be worth it when you see the picture.

Love,

Detroit, Mich.   Anabel L.

Dear Mr. President,

My mother says I have to drink three glasses of milk every day if I want to be President like you some day.

How much milk do you have to drink to just be Vice President?

Yours,

Erie, Pa.   Andrew W.

Dear President Kennedy,

May I go swimming with you in the White House pool? It would be the biggest thrill of my life.

I get off from school at 2:00 P.M. and I could come right away.

I won't be any trouble. I am a good swimmer and I will bring my own slippers and snorkel.

Yours,

Norfolk, Va.   Lester C.

President Kennedy congratulated the recipients of Young American Medals after making the formal presentation in the White House Rose Garden on June 8, 1962. The youngsters were, from left to right, Gordon B. Kilmer, age 16, of Reed City, Michigan, who saved a friend from drowning; Gerald L. Davis, age 12, from Ontario, Oregon, who rescued his two younger brothers from drowning; and Mary Ann Kingry, age 17, from Saginaw, Michigan, who had an outstanding record in the Junior Red Cross. In addition to the President, the pleased adults looking on were Robert F. Kennedy and Senator Maurine Neuberger of Oregon.

Dear President Kennedy,

Do you have any pictures of you when you were a baby? I would like to see what you looked like when you were just a kid like me.

Peter D.

Warwick, R.I.

Dear President Kennedy,

When I see you on TV, I always think you are looking right at me.

Are you? Or is it some other girl you are looking at. Marcia says you are looking at her. Who is it?

Love,
Carol C.

Clearwater, Fla.

Dear President Kennedy,

You are the best President we ever had. I like all your programs and I don't understand any of them.

Love you,
Beth G.

Teaneck, N.J.

Dear Mr. President,

I am crazy about you because you never forget the little people. I am one of the little people. I am 4 feet nine.

Harry A.

Chicago, Ill.

Dear Mr. Kennedy,

I would like to be your right-hand man. Or your left-hand man. Which job is open?

Virgil P.

New York City

Dear Mr. President,

It is my dream to be your private secretary at the White House.

I type real good. I typed this letter myself. I will bring my own typewriter and carbon paper. I never make a mistake. I am what you would call the perfect secretary.

Sincerely,

Baltimore, Md.   Alice L.

Dear President Kennedy,

If I could only sleep one night in a bed at the White House, it would be the best sleep I ever had.

I go to bed very early and I won't bother anybody.

Your friend,

Greensboro, N.C.   Eric A.

P.S. I don't even snore.

Dear President Kennedy,

Can you send me your fingerprints? If it is too much trouble, then just send me your thumbprints. I am starting a collection. Also please write where I can get fingerprints or thumbprints for these Presidents: Washington, Roosevelt, Coolidge.

Yours truly,

Pike, N.H.   William P.

Dear President Kennedy,

I have a crush on you. I hope you don't mind. I would rather you didn't mention this to anybody. Not even to the newspapers. I know you are supposed to tell them everything at the press conferences but please not this. I blush very quick.

Love,

Montgomery, Ala.   Jane W.

P.S. Please destroy this letter after you read it.

Campaigning in New York in 1960, John
Kennedy took time out from his hectic
schedule to congratulate a young bride
who had just been married at the Concord
Plaza Hotel in the Bronx, New York.

President Kennedy greeted 102 students
who visited the White House in February
1963 as the participants in the United
States Senate Youth Program. The students, representing each of the fifty
states and the District of Columbia,
spent a week in Washington studying
government procedures. The President
remarked that if one of them didn't
eventually become President, another
might "move the furniture around" in
the White House rooms as a First Lady.

Dear President Kennedy,

Please don't make any appointments for May 29th.

It is my birthday party and I think I may invite you. It is not sure yet because we may have too many boys invited but I will let you know in enough time so you can make other appointments.

My parties are always great so keep your fingers crossed.

Sincerely,

Albuquerque, N.M.   Dorothy G.

P.S. I will let you know by May 25.

Dear President Kennedy,

We had a school play and I was you. I read your Inauguration speech. Everybody said I was terrific. They said I was a great JFK. I was very proud. I am the only girl JFK in the world.

Marian H.

Anderson, Ind.

Dear President Kennedy,

There's a good chance that I will be in Washington on July 18th. If there is a good chance that you will be in Washington on July 18th, how about you and me getting together?

We have a lot to talk about. My father is a Democrat and my mother is Irish. And I'm a good talker.

Your friend,

Springfield, Ill.   Scott R.

Dear President Kennedy,

Could you please call me on the telephone some day? Nobody ever calls me. Not even the wrong number.

A pal,

Little Rock, Ark.   David F.

Hi President Kennedy,

Your barber gives you good haircuts. My barber is a butcher. After my barber cuts your hair, it looks like they ran a lawn mower over your head.

That is why I am writing this letter. If you are ever in Brooklyn stay away from the Budget Barber Shop. It's a disaster.

Your friend,

Brooklyn, N.Y.   Laurence G.

Dear President John Kennedy,

You want to trade something? I have eight bottle caps, a penknife, a good rope and a red rabbit's foot (not used).

What do you have? My sister doesn't believe that a President has anything good to trade.

You must have something.

Bertha K.

Atlanta, Ga.

Dear Mr. President Kennedy,

Will you be my valentine? I have no boyfriend. The other girls in my class all have boyfriends. Marsha has a boyfriend and his name is Stanton. Betsey has a boyfriend and his name is Larry but not me.

Please, Mr. President. You would be the best boyfriend in the whole world except for Jeffrey but he is Amy's boyfriend.

Love,

Miami, Fla.   Nancy R.

Dear President Kennedy,

I am writing to wish you a happy birthday.

Everybody should be nice to you on your birthday. Even the Republicans.

Love,

New York City   Carla P.

In November 1963, John F. Kennedy made a trip to Arlington National Cemetery accompanied by John, Jr. Little John appeared to be enjoying his military march with his father and an assortment of high-ranking generals and admirals.

Dear President Kennedy,

Boy, are you a great dresser. Where do you buy your clothes? I would like to send my boyfriend to that store. His name is Ronald. He is fourteen years old. He is never neat.

I keep telling him why don't you dress nice like JFK but Ronald says he's not President. If it is not too much trouble will you write him a letter saying it is un-American to be sloppy.

Every American should look neat like you.

Yours truly,

Wilton, Conn.   Leslie M.

Dear JFK,

I like the way you walk.
I like the way you talk.
I like the way you smile.
I like the way you think.
I like everything about you but my father voted for Nixon.

Love,

Gainesville, Ga.   Hilda G.

Dear President Kennedy,

What did you do before you were President? I never heard of you before. Were you famous before? You sure are now.

Nancy K.

Pine Bluff, Ark.

PART 5.

Dear Mrs. Kennedy

Dear Mrs. Kennedy,
   President Kennedy was a man of courage. Like the men he wrote about in his book. His courage made all the kids look up to him and admire him.
   I have courage, too, except I'm afraid to sleep in the dark.

                                                    Yours truly,
Muncie, Ind.   Howard P.

Dear Mrs. Kennedy,
   In honor of President Kennedy, I started the JFK medal in our club. It was my idea. We give the medal every year to the best boy in the club. The first medal went to me.

                                                    Yours truly,
Liberty, N.Y.   Justin K.

Dear Mrs. Kennedy,
   I have a JFK half dollar. I will cherish it forever. I will never spend it. Never. Even if I am broke. Which is all the time.

                                                    Sincerely,
Atlanta, Ga.   Henry W.

Dear Mrs. Kennedy,
   We made a whole batch of ice-cold Kool-Aid to sell to raise money for the Kennedy library.
   We didn't sell too much. I guess my father was right. Not too many people seem to want ice-cold Kool-Aid in January.

                                                    Sincerely,
Boston, Mass.   Howard L.

President and Mrs. John F. Kennedy were greeted by admiring youngsters as they left the Middleburg Community Center in Middleburg, Virginia, after they had attended mass there on April 9, 1961.

In the 1960 campaign, John F. Kennedy
signed many autographs. Here Senator
Kennedy signed the autograph book of
young Suzanne Kennedy of Mt. Morris,
Pennsylvania—no relation to the can-
didate—who seemed enchanted with Mrs.
Kennedy. With Suzanne were her sister,
Esther, 10, and the girls' father, John.

President Kennedy broke into a big smile as a small Mexican girl eluded security guards and ran to give him a farewell hug at the Mexico City airport during the Kennedys' visit to Mexico in July, 1962. The girl later received an equally cordial hug from Mrs. Kennedy.

Here the President demonstrated that he hadn't forgotten how an Eagle Scout is supposed to shake hands. He gave the left-handed Boy Scout handshake to a visiting Eagle Scout from Massachusetts who had just presented the President with a Scout membership certificate.

Dear Mrs. Kennedy,

I bought John F. Kennedy stamps because he was truly a wonderful President.

Now I have the stamps but I don't have a person to write to so I can use the John F. Kennedy stamps.

May I write to you? And could you write me back? I could write to you once a week. It won't take very long. I only have twelve stamps.

Love,

Greensboro, N.C.   Joan B.

Dear Mrs. Kennedy,

Some day I'm going to meet you and President Kennedy. I just know it. I keep wishing and hoping that I will meet you very soon.

You see, I just got a new suit that I could wear when I meet you and if I don't meet you right away, my new suit will get dirty and torn. That's what happens to all my new suits.

So if you want to meet me like I want to meet you, let's hurry up.

Best wishes,

Lowell, Mass.   Robert H.

Dear Mrs. Kennedy,

I am sitting in my room looking at this blank piece of paper and trying to think how I can tell you how much I love President Kennedy.

But I am not very good with fancy words and the more I think, the more I know that all I can say is he was the best President we ever had.

I hope you will excuse me. That is the only words I could find.

Love,

Stowe, Vt.   Rita G.

Dear Mrs. Kennedy,

I owe my friend Ritchie 8¢, Larry 4¢, Harold 3¢, Mike 2¢.

After I pay them up, I am going to send some money to the Kennedy Library.

Quincy, Mass.

Your friend,
Arnold B.

P.S. I also owe some girl 9¢.

Dear Mrs. Kennedy,

You are very lucky to be married to Mr. Kennedy.

It must be very exciting to be married to a terrific touch football player.

Raleigh, N.C.

Love,
Dotty P.

Dear Mrs. Kennedy,

I have many pictures of President Kennedy.

In my class, one boy has fifty-two pictures of President Kennedy and another boy has forty-eight. I am in third place with thirty-six pictures but I am collecting more so I can get to first place.

I will let you know when I do it.

Fairbanks, Alaska

Sincerely,
John W.

Dear Mrs. Kennedy,

When I have children, I am going to tell them all about President Kennedy.

I am writing down all the things I will tell them so I won't forget.

I won't have children for a few years because I don't even like girls yet.

Canton, Ohio

Truly yours,
Nicholas J.

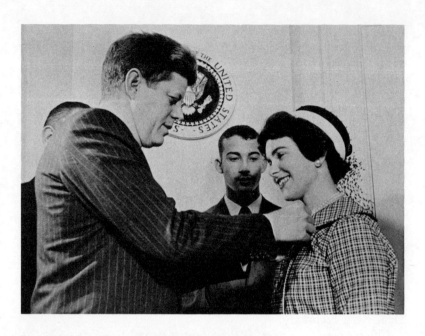

In a White House ceremony on March 23, 1961, President Kennedy presented Young American Medals for Bravery to Shirley O'Neill of San Francisco and Donald E. McGregor of Brunswick, Georgia. Completely disregarding her own safety, Shirley helped bring ashore a fellow San Francisco State College student after he had been attacked by a shark on May 7, 1959. Donald helped save the lives of a family of four by bringing to safety a cabin sloop that had gone aground during a storm on May 20, 1959.

President Kennedy carried a palm as he left Middleburg, Virginia, Community Center after attending Palm Sunday mass there on March 15, 1962. Mr. Kennedy joined his family after reviewing naval maneuvers off the North Carolina coast.

President Kennedy met members of the National High School Symphony Orchestra from the National Music Camp at Interlochen, Michigan, in August 1962. The young musicians played one of a series of musical concerts sponsored by Mrs. Kennedy that year at the White House.

Dear Mrs. Kennedy,

I want to give a million dollars to the JFK Library but I don't have a million dollars. I only have 35¢ so I am sending that instead.

Sincerely,
Rapid City, S.D.   Lawrence G.

P.S. If I ever get a million dollars I will write again.

Dear Mrs. Kennedy,

Make sure you serve President Kennedy plenty of meat and potatoes.

A President has to be very strong because he has a lot of big aggravation.

Sincerely,
Gary, Ind.   Robert B.

Dear Mrs. Kennedy,

I have written a song about President Kennedy and I would like to come to Washington and sing it for you.

My friend says it is a good song except for the words and music.

Love,
Beatrice, Neb.   Anabel R.

Dear Mrs. Kennedy,

I am writing to tell you how much we love President Kennedy. He was a good man.

My mother would write, too, but she is busy changing Patsy's diaper. She is always doing that.

Love,
Atlanta, Ga.   Dorothy R.

Dear Mrs. Kennedy,

I think President Kennedy was the greatest President that ever was President.

He was even greater than Washington and Lincoln because they were President in olden times and that doesn't count.

Your friend,

Madison, Wis.   Henry A.

Dear Mrs. Kennedy,

To make money for the Kennedy Library, we sell lemonade to all our friends.

We are making lots of money. That is because we are putting plenty of water in the lemonade and it is cheap to make.

Yours truly,

Brooklyn, N.Y.   Harold G.

Dear Mrs. Kennedy,

I am making money for the John F. Kennedy Library. The way I make the money is to shine the shoes in my family.

I will make much money for the John F. Kennedy Library because everybody always has dirty shoes in this house.

Best wishes,

Chattanooga, Tenn.   Nicky W.

Dear Mrs. Kennedy,

There is going to be a piano recital at my church on Wednesday. The piano player is me. I would like to invite you and Mr. Kennedy to come and hear me play.

I never gave a piano recital before and it would be great if you were there. I am playing beautiful music. No rock-and-roll or jazz.

Sincerely yours,

Baton Rouge, La.   Althea K.

President Kennedy chatted with a young student from Laos, one of a group of residents of Washington's International Student House. The students visited with the President in his White House office on the 25th anniversary of the International House, March 24, 1961.

President Kennedy pointed out features of the White House grounds as he met with 112 Junior Red Cross workers from 42 countries. The President spoke to the young workers briefly, and then was surprised by their rousing rendition of "For He's a Jolly Good Fellow."

Dear Mrs. Kennedy,

I believe that God is taking care of President Kennedy just like President Kennedy took care of all the people when he was President.

God knows all the good people very well.

Tulsa, Okla.

Love,
Cynthia S.

Dear Mrs. Kennedy,

I am just a little girl so I don't know much.

But even a little girl like me that doesn't know much, knows that President Kennedy was a great President.

You don't have to be a big girl to know that.

Clearwater, Fla.

Love,
Betsey G.

Dear Mrs. Kennedy,

I remember what President Kennedy said, "Ask not what your country can do for you. Ask what you can do for your country."

They were wonderful words. Could you please send me a list of the things that I could do for my country.

Albany, Ga.

Respectfully,
Mary C.

Dear Mrs. Kennedy,

My class asked me to write to tell you how much we all love President Kennedy but I can't write so good. The reason they asked me was I was the only one in the class with a five-cent stamp.

We love you.

Melissa W.

New York City

Dear Mrs. Kennedy,

I have written a play about President Kennedy. It tells all about how he was a war hero and how he became President.

The teacher says I can put my play on in school.

Would you like to play Mrs. Kennedy in my play? It is a good part. You don't have a lot to say but you are on the stage all the time.

Sincerely,

Salt Lake City, Utah   Dorothy L.

Dear Mrs. Kennedy,

Here is a drawing I made of my favorite President—JFK.

I had a little trouble with the mouth, nose and eyes. The rest I got okay.

Best wishes,

Lowell, Mass.   Linda W.

Dear Mrs. John F. Kennedy,

There have been many books written about President Kennedy but I don't believe that anyone has written a song that tells about his heroic career.

A song would be a nice way to remember him. We could sing about his many good deeds in war and peace.

One of the reasons I think a song would be good is that many people like to sing instead of reading books.

I once wrote a song about Christmas and I would like to write a song about President Kennedy. The only trouble is I can only write the words for a song and I need somebody to write the music.

If any other boy or girl writes to you and says that he wants to write the music for a song about President Kennedy, please let me know. Maybe we could get together.

Yours,

Racine, Wis.   Nicholas K. (Age 14)

Attending a Fourth of July celebration for the American colony in Mexico City in June 1962, President Kennedy talked with a Mexican girl who had just given him a bouquet of flowers. Gustavo Baz, Governor of state of Mexico, looked on.

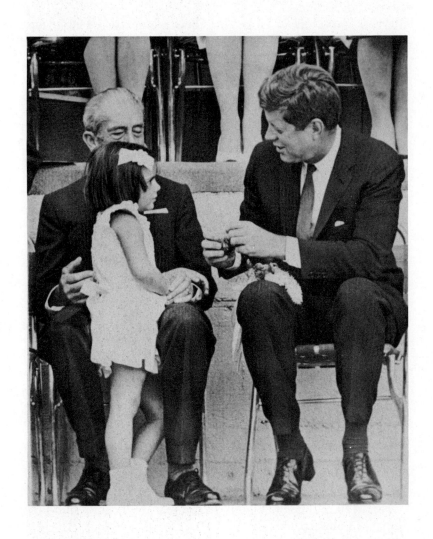

Dear Mrs. Kennedy,

We kids will never forget President Kennedy and all he has done for our country.

I am ten and I will always remember him. Even when I am a grownup and I have lots of troubles to think about.

Fargo, N.D.

Love,
Mindy C.

Dear Mrs. Kennedy,

I think they should put President Kennedy's face on Mt. Rushmore like they did with Lincoln and Washington. Then the whole world can see him.

If you can't find anybody to do it, please write me. I will go to Mt. Rushmore for the job. I have a chisel and my friends will chip in for a hammer.

Chicago, Ill.

Sincerely,
Alfred L.

Dear Mrs. Kennedy,

I have made a memory book of all the wonderful things about John F. Kennedy. I call the book *JFK Remembered*.

In the book I have his picture, a copy of the inauguration speech, an ad from the movie *PT-109*, a JFK-for-President button, a Kennedy half-dollar, the front page of *The New York Times* that announced his election and the jacket from his book *Profiles In Courage*.

I showed my memory book to some of my friends and now they are going to start one.

In a few weeks we will have 5 memory books on my block. I bet that is more *JFK Remembered* memory books than any other block in the USA.

Tarrytown, N.Y.

Sincerely,
Betsey L.

Dear Mrs. Kennedy,

I decided to save a penny for the Kennedy Library for every pound I weigh.

I weigh ninety-five pounds so I saved ninety-five pennies.

I will send the ninety-five pennies tomorrow but I will weigh myself first because today I ate pizza and maybe I gained a few pounds.

Salem, Ohio

Sincerely,
Nelson W.

Dear Mrs. Kennedy,

I told my friend Herbert that the best thing we can do to remember President Kennedy is to always be good and he asked me to write and ask if there was some other way we could remember President Kennedy.

New York City

Sincerely,
Alvin E.

Dear Mrs. John F. Kennedy,

I hate to bother you with unimportant letters but this is an important letter.

I would like very much to know what is the best way a teenage girl of 17 can honor the sacred memory of President Kennedy.

I loved President Kennedy very much and I want to do something that will be a fine tribute to his memory. But I want to do the right thing and that is why I am writing to you.

Dubuque, Iowa

Respectfully,
Aileen R.

An unusual occasion took place at the White House when quadruplets—all named Mary—visited with President Kennedy. The 16-year-old-girls, of Milton, North Carolina, are Mary Alice, Mary Louise, Mary Catherine, and Mary Anne.

Diane, 2-year-old daughter of Presidential Assistant David Powers, waved a timid goodbye to daddy's boss as the President and Powers left for a barnstorming tour in support of 1962 Democratic candidates. Mrs. Powers and son David, age nine, looked on approvingly.

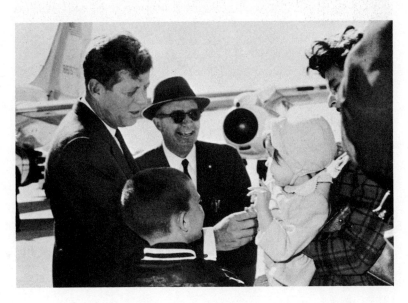

Dear Mrs. Kennedy,

In honor of John F. Kennedy, I have decided to dedicate my life to public service.

It is my hope that someday I will be worthy of the proud heritage that President Kennedy has left for young people like me.

Many years from now when I am asked what was my inspiration I will say, John F. Kennedy and his dream for a greater America.

Respectfully yours,

Louisville, Ky.   Arnold W. (Age 17)

Dear Mrs. Kennedy,

When President Kennedy came to Los Angeles during the 1960 campaign, I took a picture of him.

The picture came out but it is a little blurred. I think my hand was shaking when I took the picture because I was so excited.

I will cherish that picture forever. It means more to me than any other picture I ever took, even if it is fuzzy.

Sincerely,

Los Angeles, Calif.   Adele R.

Dear Mrs. Kennedy,

When people in foreign countries think of America, they think of John F. Kennedy.

Uncle Sam in his top hat and white beard may be the symbol of our country but to millions of people, it is the handsome, smiling face of John F. Kennedy.

I went to Paris on my vacation with my parents and all the Frenchmen I spoke to talked about JFK. I wish I could tell you everything they said but I only know a few words of French.

Yours sincerely,

Santa Rosa, Calif.   Ralph E.

Dear Mrs. Kennedy,

In New York they have named the airport the Kennedy International Airport and Cape Canaveral is now Cape Kennedy.

In every city, in every country, they are naming schools and streets and libraries after our beloved President.

My high school has already been named after a great President—Thomas Jefferson.

Even though we can't change the name of my school, we have changed the name of our civics club from the Benjamin Franklin Club to the John F. Kennedy Civics Club.

Franklin was a great man but we wanted to have our club in President Kennedy's honor because he did so much for good government.

The vote was unanimous to change the name.

Respectfully,
Milton E., President
John F. Kennedy
    Civics Club
Brooklyn, N.Y.

Dear Mrs. Kennedy,

I have a pet canary. She is a pretty canary and she is always singing.

On November 22nd, 1963, she didn't sing. She must have seen that we were very sad. Nobody in my house laughed or smiled for a long time.

It was my father who said that we must carry on for President Kennedy. That President Kennedy would have wanted us to continue to make America the greatest country in history. I will work hard for America for President Kennedy.

Sincerely,
Alex W.,
Central High School

Kenosha, Wis.

Debbie Sue Brown of Clarkston, Wash., the National March of Dimes poster girl for 1962, visited with the President at the White House on January 12, 1962, to launch the March of Dimes campaign.

Dear Mrs. Kennedy,

November 22nd, 1963 was the saddest day in history. We suffered a great loss on that day, especially teenagers.

President Kennedy was more than just a President. He was our idol. We adored him. We worshipped him. He was everything a President should be.

There will never be another President like him in a hundred years.

Yours truly,
Mindy C.

Savannah, Ga.

Dear Mrs. Kennedy,

We have learned in our history class that the good deeds that men do live after them. This is certainly true about John F. Kennedy. The history books will tell of his many deeds for the good of mankind.

In French, Spanish, German, Chinese, even Russian, they will write about his magnificent achievements.

Students a hundred years from now will praise his fine work.

John F. Kennedy has earned his place in history.

Yours very truly,
Raymond N.

Miami, Fla.

Dear Mrs. Kennedy,

In my house, we have many mementos of John F. Kennedy. We have pictures, a copy of *Profiles in Courage* and a record of all his speeches. They help us to remember President Kennedy.

Yet, even with the pictures and books and record to help us, we remember him best in our heart. He will always be there. A wonderful President who will always be first in our heart.

Sincerely,
Jennifer G.

Philadelphia, Pa.

Dear Mrs. John F. Kennedy,

There have been many beautiful tributes to John F. Kennedy by the great men of the world. I hope you'll accept my humble tribute. It comes from my heart and I mean every word of it. I am sixteen and a half.

John F. Kennedy—35th President of the United States

He was a giant among men. A ray of hope and sunshine in a dark world. He made the weak feel strong and gave hope to the poor and downhearted.

He stood for all that was good and fine and wonderful. He was a man of charm and warmth and good humor. He served his country and his countrymen bravely in peace and war. Children loved him. He made the world a better place to live. He will not be forgotten. His name will live forever as one of the best men God ever put on this earth.

Respectfully submitted,

North Platte, Neb.   Ann B.

Dear Mrs. Kennedy,

President Kennedy was loved by America and all the world. He was loved as a President and a man.

The world loved him because he was honest and fair to every country big and small.

America loved him because he was an inspiration and gave us courage.

America and the world lost one of their great men and I lost a friend.

Yours truly,

Cumberland, Md.   Raymond N.

President Kennedy, who enjoyed a repu-
tation as an amateur football player,
showed his passing grip on a ball given
to him by members of the Pennsylvania
State team. The football players were
obviously impressed by the President's
technique, and the President enjoyed
his few moments off from official duty
to talk with fellow football players.

Edward Korry, Ambassador-designate to
Ethiopia, introduced his young daughter
Alexandra, 4, to President Kennedy, as
the other Korry children—Deborah, 7,
Edward Jr., 9, and Patricia, 11—waited
their turns. The family called on the
President on March 13, 1963, the date
of Mr. Korry's swearing-in ceremonies.

Dear Mrs. Kennedy,
  I hope you like my poem:
  His name was John F. Kennedy,
  A great President of the USA.
  His name was John F. Kennedy,
  He worked for us each day.
  His name was John F. Kennedy,
  And he was loved in every state.
  His name was John F. Kennedy,
  A President strong, handsome and great.

                              Sincerely,
                              Louise H.,
Evansville, Ind.   Evansville High School